THE BURNING BUSH

Poems from Modern Israel

THE BURNING BUSH

Poems from Modern Israel

Edited by
Moshe Dor and Natan Zach

Introduction by
Alan Sillitoe

W. H. Allen · London
A Howard & Wyndham Company
1977

Printed and bound in Great Britain by Butler & Tanner Ltd, Frome & London, for the Publishers, W. H. Allen & Co Ltd, 44 Hill Street, London W1X 8LB

ISBN 0 491 02461 4

Contents

EDITORS' NOTE

'And people who left whole are brought home in the evening, like small change' (Amichai). Words that speak of death – to quote another poet represented in this collection – are rarely absent from the writings of younger Israeli poets. In its seemingly prosaic, underplaying manner, Amichai's simile is equally characteristic. Recent Hebrew poetry has lost the innocence and self-confidence that made possible the high-flown rhetoric of some earlier poets. 'The age of the first crocus will never return.'

The Burning Bush is not one more comprehensive anthology of *poets*. Rather, in its focus on war and its 'grammar of fears', on loss and survival, the time-bound realities of conflict and a timeless Jerusalem, this collection of *poems* highlights some of the major themes of contemporary Hebrew literature, as well as representing a sensibility which, even in its most private experiences, has never been allowed to forget the newspaper headlines. Of the thirty-three poets, a few made their appearance shortly before or during the Second World War and the Holocaust, but most of them have published their first poems since Israel's War of Independence in 1948.

We would like to express our thanks to Alan Sillitoe and Anthony Rudolf who not only read the manuscript and commented on it, but also translated some of the poems and gave advice concerning others.

Thanks are due to Nili Cohen and the Institute for Translation of Hebrew Literature for their support; and to the authors and translators for their agreement to be included in this collection.

The poems of Samih El-Kassim and Siham Dawoud, both Israeli Arab poets, were translated from the Arabic. Those of Robert Friend and Dennis Silk were originally written in English. Most of Avot Yeshurun's poems are included in *The Collection* (Poems 1964–1976), selected, translated and with a foreword by Harold Schimmel.

Moshe Dor   Natan Zach   1 March 1977

INTRODUCTION TO ISRAELI POETRY

Poetry is a major part of modern Israeli literature. This present selection shows that poetry in Israel is in the process of completing its occupation of that fully-charged and explosive meeting ground between God and Man – often secular with its show of respect, but nearly always religious in its inspiration. A poet stops short of becoming a priest when it seems that the used gift might err too much on the side of wisdom, a quality which could then impair a sense of speculation on the one hand, and possibly sever an attachment to nature on the other. In this matter the subconscious works efficiently, and the poet stays nearer to the fundamental experiences of humanity rather than aspiring to approach the metaphysical spaces of God. A poet searches only to the extent that he or she will not risk getting lost; asks rather than answers; writes poems rather than intones those speculations which would cause him to lose direction among the finally indefinable spaces of metaphysics.

And yet a poet must believe that it is possible to speak directly to God, with no one to intercede, or interfere, or distort the words in any way. King David, as a poet, called himself 'the apple of God's eye', the fruit of the eye of God for all his people to behold and, if possible, emulate. This image from Psalm Seventeen leads one to observe that a poet is everybody's eye, that he or she can be the eye of a whole country, and even, at times, the eye of the world. The poet interprets Man to God, whereas the priest interprets God to Man. No one can truly do both. God, Poet, Humanity, make a threeway network of the spirit.

With one or two exceptions all these poems have been translated from Hebrew. It hardly needs pointing out that the themes are very much of the land and of the people from which they originate. That is to say, they are the same themes as from any other land, but

7

with the additional colour and depth given to them by the Land of the Bible. This inescapable and forceful fact must redouble the interest of this selection for anyone who considers a large part of his culture to be based upon that of the Bible. Reading these poems one enjoys the images of Biblical landscape, savours the thoughts of its Biblical people, as well as appreciates the tribulations of Modern Israel.

The number of times God is mentioned are legion, the sense of religion strong. It could not have been otherwise, nor should it have been. *A Place Of Fire* by Zelda, has in it the lines:

'... mercy for us
from Him who is above all.'

which echoes the melodious free-verse from the Psalms. And later in the same poem she remarks on:

'... our terrible love
for the City of David' –

which recalls the language of Isaiah – as does Meir Wieseltier's *A Dream of Death as an Angel*.

Other poems have as their themes the survival from the Holocaust, and the Return to Israel. Some – especially the beautiful poems of Dalya Ravikovich – are about love. But many, as one would expect from Israel, try to come to terms with the disorientation and ferocity of war. Specially noteworthy are the poems by Dennis Silk (*Sleeping gun-crew*), Tuvia Ruebner (*Among Iron Fragments*), Yehuda Amichai (*Rain on the Battlefield*), and Moshe Dor (*War*). They try to define the experience of mortal combat, and in some measure succeed, but there is no final definition of war without eternal peace, and what country has ever been able to claim that?

8

These poems are notable also in that they belong to the heart and not the head, to a priceless and eternal reality, and not to fantasy experiences. The personal poems are firmly rooted. Simple and ordinary statements in T. Carmi's *A view of Jerusalem* send out influence in concentric circles:

> *'Child, child, little flower,*
> *can I already play with you at words?'*

The complexities in this one seem endless.

They are from a language in transition, a Hebrew searching for runways from which to take off into its full modern flowering. The restlessness is apparent in even this small number of poems. A language which stood more or less still for so long, though used in the schools and synagogues scattered around the world, has once more acquired movement and a desire for development because it is again in the land which gave it birth, and where the bedrock of its heritage was formed.

Alan Sillitoe
10 December 1976

9

List of Poets and
Biographical Notes

Avot Yeshurun: born 1904 in Poland. In Israel since 1925. First poem published in 1934.

Zerubavel Gilead: born 1912 in Bessarabia. In Israel since 1922. Began publishing in 1929.

Robert Friend: born 1913 in New York. In Israel since 1950. First book published in 1941.

David Rokeah: born 1916 in Poland. In Israel since 1934. Began publishing in 1935.

Amir Gilboa: born 1917 in the Ukraine. In Israel since 1937. Began publishing in 1941.

Abba Kovner: born 1918 in Russia. In Israel since 1945. Began publishing at the outbreak of World War Two.

Yechiel Mar: born 1921 in Poland. In Israel since 1937. First book published 1951. Died 1969.

Chaim Guri: born 1923 in Tel Aviv, Israel. Began publishing in 1943.

Zelda: born 1924 in Russia. In Israel since her late twenties. First book published 1967.

Anadad Eldan: born 1924 in Poland. In Israel since 1934. Began publishing in 1953.

Tuvia Ruebner: born 1924 in Slovakia. In Israel since 1941. Began publishing in 1953.

Yehuda Amichai: born 1924 in Germany. In Israel since 1936. Began publishing in the late 1940's.

T. Carmi: born 1925 in New York. In Israel since 1947. First book published in 1950.

Avner Treinin: born 1928 in Tel Aviv. Began publishing in 1947.

Dennis Silk: born 1928 in London. In Israel since 1955.

Pinchas Sadeh: born 1929 in Poland. In Israel since 1934. Began publishing in 1945.

Aryeh Sivan: born 1929 in Tel Aviv. Began publishing in 1948.

Dan Pagis: born 1930 in Rumania. In Israel since 1947. Began publishing in 1949.

Moshe Ben Shaul: born 1930 in Jerusalem. First book published in 1954.

Natan Zach: born 1930 in Germany. In Israel since 1935. Began publishing in 1951.

Moshe Dor: born 1932 in Tel Aviv. First book published in 1954.

Itamar Yaoz-Kest: born 1934 in Hungary. In Israel since 1951. Began publishing in 1954.

David Avidan: born 1934 in Tel Aviv. First book published in 1954.

Israel Pincas: born 1935 in Bulgaria. In Israel since 1941. Began publishing in 1961.

Moshe Hane'omi: born 1935 in Tel Aviv. Began publishing in 1961.

Dalya Ravikovich: born 1936 in Ramat-Gan, Israel. First book published in 1963.

Samih El-Kassim: born 1939 in Zorqa (then Transjordan). Began publishing in the late 1950's.

Yair Hurwitz: born 1941 in Tel Aviv. First book published in 1961.

Meir Wieseltier: born 1941 in Moscow. In Israel since 1949. First book published in 1963.

Chaim Be'er: born 1945 in Jerusalem. First book published in 1970.

Yisrael Hame'iri: born 1948 in Israel.

Siham Dawoud: born 1951 in Ramleh, Israel. She began publishing in 1969.

Be'eri Hazak: born in Kibbutz Afikim. Killed in action on the Suez Canal, October 1973.

List of Translators

Reuven Ben-Yosef (Sadeh), Avraham Birman (Ben Shaul, Wieseltier, Zach), Chana Bloch (Ravikovich), S. F. Chyet (Hurwitz), Marcia Falk (Zelda), Elaine Feinstein (Zach), Richard Flantz (Wieseltier, El-Kassim), Robert Friend (Pagis, Gilead, Ruebner), Leonore Gordon (Hurwitz), Assia Gutman (Amichai), Michael Hamburger (Rokeah), A. C. Jacobs (Gilboa, Hane'omi, Amichai, Hame'iri), Denis Johnson (Dor), Shirley Kaufman (Treinin, Kovner, Wieseltier), Aharon Megged (Hazak), Stephen Mitchell (Pagis, Be'er, Carmi), Dom Moraes (Kovner, Guri), Uzi Nystar (Yaoz-Kest, Guri), Shlomit Rimmon (Wieseltier, Kovner), Anthony Rudolf (Sivan, Eldan, Zelda), Harold Schimmel (Pincas, Ravikovich, Amichai, Yeshurun, Ruebner), Bat-Sheva Sheriff (Mar), Jon Silkin (Gilboa, Zach, Mar), Alan Sillitoe (Avidan, Hazak, Amichai, Dawoud), Sasson Somekh (El-Kassim), Natan Zach (Sivan, Eldan, Zelda), John Batki (Dor).

Avot Yeshurun

The Jews

From a steep booth,
In a great simile,
That went bodily,
Like *Zahal.**

According to this
Formulation we fix:
'People will be crushed
Under us and nations

Under our feet.'
Gentile brethren
Say with
God our God.

For the honour of the Presence
And the honour of the Law
And the honour of the feast.
Our feast.

From star-times in their orbit,
From time of their worship in other times,
Jews alone
In the Middle East.

From time of eyes split
To understanding. From lid
Of stars for armies.
From star-times in their orbit.

From times of star speech
To their sects then.
From global revolution
For the Galaxy.

* *Zahal:* Zva Hagana l'Yisrael, or the Israel Defence
Forces. (H.S.)

From tyrannical times
of the *Hixos*
With *Gewalts*
Of nakedness.

From star-times in their orbit.
From naked time. From times alone
In the Levant. From the end of time,
From star-times in their orbit.

A man is afraid
Of himself on the road.
A man'll say
Things to

Himself scare.
'll say, 'll say
a man'll, and forgetting
What people.

The King hath brought me
Into a warm room
Of a winged song
Of the Jews.

A man fears
Himself. 'll say
A man, & forget
Whát people.

The Lord is close
To the heart *broken*.
The King kills
& quickens.

You lóved us?
You wánted us?
Make for us
An Ecumenical Council. Yes.

Yeho' bless us
In the Middle East.
Not a man with us
In the Middle East.

The Jews who are heavy
Like boot leather.
The Jews who are learnéd
And learnéd, and heavy.

The Jews who are deep
In boot leather,
As they move from place
To place, swearing.

The sworn and knowledgeable
In boot matters,
In the folds of leather,
In the fall of leathery-leather.

Those boots
That silenced your going,
May they be worthy the infiltration
Delicate, of the poem.

Translated by Harold Schimmel

Avot Yeshurun

From *Thirty Pages of Avot Yeshurun*

1

The day will come no one will read my Mother's
    letters.
I have, of them, a packet.
No one's
no words.

The day will come no one will care to take them.
A bundleful to spare.
They'll say: paper
scraps, alack.

That day I'll bring them to Bar Kochba's cave
to send them up in dust. No ancient world
will probe her
Mother tongue.

3

Before you a beggar   no feet on him sprouted.
He'll walk on his hands in the broil.
His hands are night's quiver;
afternoons meagre.

Yonas ducks by me all skin & bones.
D'you know what *eats* Yonas?
A milli-million bones.
Unbelievable.

The Fatman from *Dizengoff** hogs a whole bench.
D'you know what he told Job?
You weren't so fat
Mas'er Job.

* Tel Aviv street of outdoor cafés. (H.S.)

6
I wrote a diary, wrote two days, three, I quote:
Here am I one day, two days,
three, after two thousand
virtually, years.

I came to the Land, ate days & figcakes, honey-on-
　　the-tongue.
Scratchy figcakes, sticky tongue.
My means for sleep
on interrupted eating.

My diary lost, I worked two days, three,
　　consecutively.
The out-of-work work two.
I took another figcake
& my guts growled.

7
I got your letter & in it answer answer.
Until the postman in his glory
dew daubs the eyes.
Answer answer.

I answered with a letter & in it enviable riches
acacia & shamuti-orange trees.
Now I must answer.
Answer answer.

I had not one good word from home.
Your letter doesn't mention me.
Just now the sun passed over.
Answer answer.

Translated by Harold Schimmel

Avot Yeshurun

Stampless

My kid	brother
found	hisself
a Jewish	National Fund
stamp.	I snitched it
for me.	At day
break	it ended
with him.	At mid
night	transferred
to me.	Slinked
to him,	skulked
to me.	Roved
to him,	robbed
to me.	Oozed
to him,	stole
to me.	Sacked
with me,	stuck
with him.	Gyrated
so	it wept
to me.	No boundary
twixt him	& me.
No	stamp
& no	collector.

Translated by Harold Schimmel

Avot Yeshurun

The Syrian–African Rift*

The poem on the eve of this day

The sages say, that at the time the Syrian–African
      Rift
occurred, the celestial inhabitants were not
up-to-date. Each man was engaged
at his trade. In grinding hatchets. In splitting
      beasts.

Ancient humanity and land of the axe.
And when those wanted some change on the earth
they had to do it by putting to sleep.
After that they waken the earth.

Like they did to me once in isolation in narcosis
under the plywood and the roof
in Belinson Hospital: 'Yeshurun, you underwent an
      operation!'
And here I am. Yom Kippur.

* *The Syrian–African Rift:* A geological formation which, on
Israel's side, extends from the Huleh region, through Lake Kin-
nereth, down the Jordan Valley and the Dead Sea to Eilat and
the Red Sea.
    The background of this group of six poems is the October or
Yom Kippur War of 1973. The surprise attack found two thirds
of the nation in synagogue. The major part of the call-up consisted
in locating the particular synagogue of the reservist and pulling
him out as quickly as possible without overly disrupting the ser-
vice. (H.S.)

Avot Yeshurun

The poem on the Jews

The head of the congregation here stands at the
    head
of a long line of congregants who stand behind
    him.
A longer line than the one that departed and isn't.
Which – someone who has not seen it,

gradually the sight eludes him whereas
those other people, if not to resort to inhuman
idioms, why it can be said
with one word: they were the big ones when we
    were small.

At their hands each thing was cut they even cut
our slices of bread and they cut us
half an apple which voice of the apple we heard at
    the cutting.
And touched our cheeks and called our names.

They were in a closed circuit the masculine Jews
    we adored.
On holidays and on Sabbaths. With force they
    conducted
prayers and chanted hymns and acknowledged
    God.
And when Yom Kippur came kept packages of
    food for us at the fast.

After the holiday we still longed for the same
    holiday and
the same Jews to see them together. It's good to be
    among those who are one
people who neither change 'nor all their wrath
    awaken' and look
upon me as someone they didn't see awhile.

Translated by Harold Schimmel

22

Avot Yeshurun

The poem on this day

He stood before the prayer and before the singing.
I stood before the threshold. Someone bursts out:
Is there a shelter here?
There's a war here.

Plump a door opens.
I'm before the threshold. This
day, on which I was born
before 'Closing Prayer',

Yom Kippur. It's between us.
Romeo-and-Juliet-cinema photographers,
now foreign correspondents, will formally launch
   it:
Yom Kippur or Day of Judgement*.

Rabbi Shmuel Eliahu of Modzitz apportions his
   tear to men.
He stood in prayer and singing.
I noticed that. I beat palm to palm, and came out
   singing.

Translated by Harold Schimmel

----

* A journalistic dilemma of christening. These two names
competed in the communications during the early weeks of
the war, the former eventually winning out. (H.S.)

Avot Yeshurun

The poem on the guilt

Blest be Mother bind your hand on my head on
   the eve
of this day. I would have what would I have done
for Yom Kippur. Forests crash and you inside and
   at the center
of the land your soul and body you longed and did
   not arrive.

Your Father came in a dream to you.
Opened the glass cupboard; broke you a glass. A
   child of yours died
and you asked why. Your Father didn't reply and
   went out and you meant to forgive
and lay on the floor and lay on the child and died
   of longing.

Translated by Harold Schimmel

Avot Yeshurun

The poem on the Africs

Plump a door opens. A soldier pulled a reservist
  outside.
Straightened the *tallith** from street to street and
  listening to the soldier's story.
Walked with the soldier cat and cat
and cheek and cheek.

The two reservist guys went to the Syrian—
African Rift: You came to us to escape the white.
But you be the villain? Loathsome to me is death
because Afric's in your grip.

We have a problem of a sacrifice of Isaac.
And yours, you're inclined to think, the sacrifice of
  Isaac.
For us it comes out as a father has mercy on
  children.
For you it comes out as a father has mercy on
  himself.

Translated by Harold Schimmel

---

* 'Tallith', the prayer shawl, usually worn in the synagogue;
now seen in the streets, as soldiers already in uniform were
pumped for information by the congregants. There is no
newspaper or radio broadcasting on Yom Kippur in Israel. (H.S.)

Avot Yeshurun

The poem on our Mother, Our Mother Rachel

And the two reservist guys went. Look, don't
  shoot.
And Jacob lifted his legs and went to the land of
  B'nei Kedem.
And Jacob said unto them: Ben Gurion and
  Nechemia Argov, my brothers, from Whence?*
From Ben Gurion and Nechemia Argov no reaction
  no response and the two went off.

Ben Zvi's shack† a wooden candelabrum
of local make carvings by Batia Lishanski††,
and not a painting on every painting and not
  Chagall
on every France and presidential mansion rejoice
  and rejoice.

Inside sits Jacob
Esau stands outside.
From the window looks and wails
Esau's mother from the lattice.

Punished Earth.
You needn't start up with her. To speak
of her you need. To trick out her wardrobe. As
  meadows
wore sheep so we wore that Land.

---

 * Biblical Jacob confuses the 1970's reservists for the late
Prime Minister and his secretary of the fifties.
 † Former President Yitzchak Ben Zvi had a knotty-pine
annex to his house which served as an official reception room.
The furnishings were homely, true to the tenor of the State in
the early years. The late President Ben Zvi was known to
enter a Jerusalem cinema unaccompanied and on the spur of
the moment.
 †† Israeli sculptress. (H.S.).

Don't call her by many names.
Call her Rachel.
A man is born as a child and dies as a child.
All this close to the mother.

Punished Earth.
You needn't start up with her. To speak
of her you need. To trick out. As meadows
so we wore this Land.

Translated by Harold Schimmel

Zerubavel Gilead

Wild goose

The distance is sealed with lead;
The light is strange and chill;
The wind counts endlessly
The leaves that fall on the hill.

Harsh is this season that will
Endure no blue disguise.
A bird, like an outlaw, finds
No haven in its cold skies.

Tossing in wind and cloud,
With neck outstretched it flees,
Burns over forests, and cries
Wildly across the seas.

It breaks, by a crooning stream,
At the threshold of dark, its flight,
To leap with heart renewed
Into the heart of night:

To breast whatever befall—
Greenness of lawn or flood.
A star snapped off from the sky,
It streams like a jet of blood.

But morning beholds a bird
That preens with a sleepy bill.
And the wind counts, endlessly
The leaves that fall on the hill.

Translated by Robert Friend

Robert Friend

Soliloquy of the King

I
My soldiers are at the doors,
my guards at the windows.
On the roofs of the city
binocular telescope radar
are doing their duty.
A sleepless militia
are glued to the microscopes.

How can he enter?

The FBI have grilled
the underground streams,
and G-men frisk
suspicious pockets of air.
Special agents
look down the mouth
of every road.

Where can he enter?

Official seers
have been assigned to clouds.

Peering a thousand ways,
eyes of potatoes watch.
Eyes of needles pierce
out of strategic haystacks.

Which way are the sunflowers turning?

II
I trust nothing and no one.

I no longer believe
in my sceptre and my crown.
I have seen the rust
fretting at the edges.

Help me!
My diamonds cloud,
my opals curdle.

Unravel the spider webs,
peel the mirrors,
dissolve the shadows.
Help me!

Dear Dr. Wisdom,
disarm him with an argument.
Good Bishop Boneless,
manacle him with a miracle.
Strong Simple Simon,
chop off his head.

Not even they can help me —
my sweet fools
studying all day
an image's image
afloat in the fountain.

I want my dinner!

The worms will digest it.

Tell the cooks
to bring me baser fare. Ha. ha!

Help!

My blood is a traitor.
My veins conspire against me.
My heart and my kidneys
have signed a secret treaty.
My teeth bite hungrily
towards my last supper.

David Rokeah

From my diary

I
My groping is no accident. I learn each day
from the crabs on the shore
how to scuttle for cover. My nets do not flutter
like flags on the roof. Today is a holiday
for the poem whose rhyme has lost itself in rhyme.

II
Meanwhile it is summer
and the sea roars at the window
like a bursting dam. I forget your questions
that keep returning like last year's rain.
The peaches are ripe but no girl picks them.

III
Burrow, burrow deep in layers of salt
and sulphur. From conches that calcine
white coal grows. I am impatient
for the time when the moon races the sea.

IV
I stand yet, a sentry on the wall,
in my hand an hourglass, in my eye the eye of a
    fish
caught on your hook – and already the skyline
    clouds
like a mountain – and already night in your doorway
like a beggar in a scarlet cloak.

V
Alone with the counterweights of longing
you will gather the ashes of lightning
when it has charged the sea.
Your dead loves
are in these ashes.

VI
Only the autumn night, abroad, will decide the goal
    of your love
your words will take the meaning of marks in
    stone,
your deeds of ripening fruit –
by every route your straying will take you home
to Jerusalem.

Translated by Michael Hamburger

Amir Gilboa

And my brother was silent

From *Ancient war*

My brother came back from the field
In grey clothing.
And I was afraid my dream would be false
And began at once to count his wounds.
And my brother was silent.

Then I burrowed into the pockets of his tunic
And found a dressing with a dried stain,
And on a crumpled postcard his girl's name
Beneath a picture of some poppies.
And my brother was silent.

And I undid his bundle
And took out his things, memory after memory.

Hurray, my brother, my *heroic* brother,
Look I've found your symbols!
Hurray, my brother, my *heroic* brother,
   I'll shout your praises!

And my brother was silent.
And my brother was silent.

And his blood cried out of the ground.

Translated by A. C. Jacobs

·Amir Gilboa

In the distance guns thundered

The cellar was damp and deep.
People crammed it full.
Through the shrieking of babies
An old man cried out
Our God would prevail.

Then a hush descended
As happens
In life and in books.
In the distance guns thundered.
Somebody said:
They are making the town a rubbish heap.

After that there was a long silence.
Suddenly one of the women
Began screaming
There was someone wounded at the entrance
To the cellar.
A knife slash of pain cut the air.

Someone opened the door for the first time
And said: It's a dog.

Everyone let out a breath of relief.
My throat was choking.
The wax candle dripped its tears.

Translated by A. C. Jacobs

Amir Gilboa

Isaac

In the early morning the sun walked through the
Forest
With father and me
My right hand in his left.

A knife like lightning burned between the trees
And I am so frightened at the fear in my eyes
Of the sight of blood on the leaves.

Father father hurry and save Isaac so that
No one is missing from the noonday meal.

It is me that's butchered, son
And my blood already on the leaves,
Father's voice was cut across,
His face, pale.

I wanted to scream, writhing, so as not to
Believe;
Pulling my eyes open.
And awoke.

And my right hand
Lacked its blood.

Translated by Natan Zach and Jon Silkin

Abba Kovner

It's late

Naked soil is the way to my beloved.
I come to her like someone coming to a tryst.
I quietly try to rebuild
a city, transparent. To sail confused houses
in two-way streets. To give them back
their faces, to arrange
rotating crops, to let the sea
break through into the small square
rooms and wash the frost flowers
and send stripes alternately from the windows
like an old-fashioned devoted servant. Already
there is a road.
A road sign.
It's really possible to go. I will only hang
my hat on the acacia branch
to sway, I will set
my eyes in the new streetlights so they will not
     close
in difficult moments. In the neck of the weather
     vane
I have already tied my tie
with the pure gold pin
I inherited from my father. I will spread
my shirt before the first policeman's
dog who will come on time
running in front of his master. And my shoes
I will leave my shoes
for the cat
until a better story will be found
for the city children
and you
only you, my little sister, will I take with me
on my back. To carry you beyond
my naked plot of soil.

Translated by Shirley Kaufman

Abba Kovner

Nearby music

I bought my son a little bell.
He favours his left hand. I set
The little bell upon his palm.
With his left hand he clattered it,

Throughout the world you will find bells.
Now the frogs croak, not for prey.
When my son rings his little bell,
Tamar and Amnon through the evening sigh.

And I by night saw a strange forest –
Beautiful were the bewildered eyes of the ram.
A bell is clattering, clashing on his breast.
The barbed wire fence is chasing him.

The walls are thick, the houses won't explain.
Perhaps the brilliant sea will understand
The sprouting of the ashes in the plain.

My son, don't cry. The ram's pride suffered all.
Clatter the little bell in your right hand.
I shall stay with you here until nightfall.

Translated by Dom Moraes

Abba Kovner

There's no man without a clock

There's no man without an alarm clock
on his table
or in his blood. After the defeat
I entered my room and closed myself in.
Until I made up my mind
I did not bolt the door.
When I made up my mind
I could not force myself to lock up
my house, and bolt the door.
From the city chained in its twilight
a strange fragrance burst as the clock
rang like a riot. My daughter!
I expected the door to open – but the clock
like a bird call strong without meaning
rings
and rings
– does nobody hear it but me?

Translated by Shirley Kaufman and Shlomit Rimmon

Abba Kovner

They build houses in Ein Hahoresh

They build houses in Ein Hahoresh just like the
    rest of the world.
First they lay a foundation,
they add walls, and finally
they pour the reinforced concrete roof.
Maybe it's crazy, but I'll try
with my own hands, maybe
in my last years,
to build another house. First I'll pour concrete
the size of my body, without doors.
I'll install a window
(why do they leave the windows for the end?)
and if I don't have a big enough foundation
for my head,
I'll call through the window
to you, my love.

Translated by Shirley Kaufman

Yechiel Mar

An appended poem

He who left in the very early
morning, has passed, and disappeared.
And despite our requests
and secret gifts made
so that he exert himself
in the capital, for us,
he has forgotten our case.

We are left with none
to look to our affairs.
It's true: we sent clouds,
a few of them, to jog
him – and only one
returned; an empty pail.
There's none now to hand him the
petitions of our crying silence.

Each morning I look out for
your coming to the city;
nothing in me moves.
Each noon I climb the tower.
Maybe something will break in me.
Evening comes, feeling dry
as copper. I retreat inside me.

Translated by Bat-Sheva Sheriff and Jon Silkin

Yechiel Mar

Hope

My hope is: that you hear.
I know
that it holds little.
So they told me.
Even so, I want
to hope again for this.
That you hear how I hope:

My hope is like a hind, waiting.
Be careful
not to embrace it. Break one dry
shoot of a tree, and it goes.
And would we have the strength
for another beginning?

I hope and am that hope.

Translated by Bat-Sheva Sheriff and Jon Silkin

Chaim Guri

Lands of immigration

And the ship kisses the warm quay
And I too am there.
I was not pitched overboard to appease the fish of
    the sea.

A still sea of ink.
A moon over the sea
One by one they move into death, the remembered
    things.

And the ship kisses the quay,
Illumined, beautiful,
And all that has not been
Shall be, if God wills it.

I have borrowed their secret of strength from those
    who hope
And I shall repay at the proper time,
Without interest, with the white from my head
And the rasping of my chest.

And the ship kisses the warm quay,
Blind customs officers count their dues,
We may achieve our phoenix hour, today.

And the ship slowly kisses the strange quay.
There was a time, I remember, when I longed
To sweep the gates of Gaza before me.

All I created lives.
– I and no God, I and no angel –

From my compassion and my dream
I can furnish iron rations for those
About to make a long farewell at last.

And the ship kisses the living quay.
For there is no threshold where a body does not
   rest.

But I tell you this:
No thief has taken
Your right to be reborn.
My fools, in the first boat that sails,
Embark for the new land of gold.

The ship kisses the good quay.
The man comes down, and the earth rushes
   towards him.

Translated by Dom Moraes

Chaim Guri

Heritage

The ram came last of all.
Abraham did not know it replied
To what his child had asked before –
First of his strength as his days died.

The old head, lifting, saw
It was no dream he had dreamt.
Before him stood the angel.
Clattering, the knife fell.

Released from the cords, the child
Stared at his father's back.

Isaac, they say, escaped the sacrifice.
So he lived long and with luck
Till he grew weak in the eyes.

But he bequeathed, to his offspring, that hour of
    his life.
And, when they are born, in their hearts
Is a knife.

Translated by Dom Moraes

Chaim Guri

His mother

Years ago, at the end of the Song of Deborah,
I heard the stillness of Sisera's delayed chariot.
I saw Sisera's mother standing at the window,
Silver streaking her hair.

A blaze of embroidery,
The girls saw embroidered cloth of captive necks.
That same hour he lay in the tent as if sleeping,
His hands quite empty.
On his chin traces of butter, milk and blood.

The silence was not broken by horses and chariots.
One after another the girls too fell silent.
My silence touched theirs.
After a while the sun went down.
After a while twilight went away.

For forty years the land had rest. For forty years
No racing horses or dead ghostly-eyed horsemen.
But she died, soon after her son's death.

Translated by Uzi Nystar

Anadad Eldan

The words that speak of death

The words that speak of death
are frail and blind like chance.
The words that speak of death
drift slow as bubbles
through the fine veins of the heart.

Words you wrote in green
quietly implore
while the sunflower
turns its face.

The words that speak of death
are low as grass.

Wind in the reeds:
it is not words that speak of death.

Translated by Anthony Rudolf and Natan Zach

Zelda

Everyone has a name

Everyone has a name
given to him by God
and given to him by his parents
Everyone has a name
given to him by his stature
and the way he smiles
and given to him by his clothing
Everyone has a name
given to him by the mountains
and given to him by his walls
Everyone has a name
given to him by the stars
and given to him by his neighbours
Everyone has a name
given to him by his sins
and given to him by his longing
Everyone has a name
given to him by his enemies
and given to him by his love
Everyone has a name
given to him by his holidays
and given to him by his work
Everyone has a name
given to him by the seasons
and given to him by his blindness
Everyone has a name
given to him by the sea
and given to him
by his death.

Translated by Marcia Falk

Zelda

I stood in Jerusalem

I stood
in Jerusalem,
Jerusalem suspended from a cloud,
in a graveyard with people crying
and a crooked tree.
Blurry mountains
and a tower.
You are not!
death spoke to us.
You are not!
he turned to me.

I stood
in the midst of Jerusalem,
Jerusalem checkered in the sun,
smiling like a bride in the field,
slender green grass
by her side.

Why were you frightened
yesterday in the rain?
death spoke to me.
Am I not your quiet
older brother?

Translated by Marcia Falk

Zelda

A place of fire

Mountain air alive
beloved breathing
ask mercy for us
from Him who is above all.
A place of fire,
a place of crying,
a place of madness —
the bridegroom and his bride
ask the mercy of heaven
that the horizon
does not simply fall apart.
Dogs and cats are terrified.
Only in what grows
do the juices remain
unpolluted
a step from the abyss,
only in the flowers
does the sweetness not retreat
one step from death.
For that which grows
is a different race from us,
except for the olive trees
sad and wise like people.
And when a king
alien and hostile
sullies our affinity
to the city
whose neck a loving prophet
adorned with sapphires,
turquoise and jacinth —
the silver tree-tops
tremble like my heart,
and when a king
alien and hostile
sullies our terrible love
for the City of David,

the roots
of the olive tree hear
the small soldier's blood
murmur in the dust;
the city
lies heavy on my life.

Translated by Anthony Rudolf and Natan Zach

Yehuda Amichai

Out of three or four in a room

Out of three or four in a room
One is always standing at the window.
Forced to see the injustice amongst the thorns,
The fires on the hill.

And people who left whole
Are brought home in the evening, like small
    change.

Out of three or four in a room
One is always standing at the window.
Hair dark above his thoughts.
Behind him, the words.
And in front of him the words, wandering, without
    luggage,
Hearts without provision, prophecies without water
And big stones put there
And staying, closed like letters
With no addresses; and no one to receive them.

Translated by Assia Gutman

Yehuda Amichai

God has pity on kindergarten children

God has pity on children in kindergartens,
He pities school children – less.
But adults he pities not at all.

He abandons them,
And sometimes they have to crawl on all fours
In the roasting sand
To reach the dressing station,
And they are streaming with blood.

But perhaps
He will have pity on those who love truly
And take care of them
And shade them
Like a tree over the sleeper on the public bench.

Perhaps even we will spend on them
Our last pennies of kindness
Inherited from mother,

So that their own happiness will protect us
Now and on other days.

Translated by Assia Gutman

Yehuda Amichai

Psalm

A song on a day
some building contractor
cheated me. A psalm.
Plaster falls from the ceiling,
the wall is sick, paint cracks like lips.

The vines I've sat under, the fig tree,
all are words. The rustling of leaves
gives an illusion of God and of justice.

I dip my dry look
like bread into the softening death
that is always on the table before me.
Already my life has turned
my life into a revolving door.
I think of those who, in happiness and success,
have left me behind, those
who like pampered and brilliant grapes
are carried for show between two
and those who are also carried
between two and they are wounded or dead. A
    psalm.

When I was a child I sang in the synagogue choir,
I sang until my voice broke. I sang
first voice and second voice. I'll sing
until my heart breaks, first heart and second heart.
A psalm.

Translated by Harold Schimmel

Yehuda Amichai

Rain on the battlefield

Rain falls on friends' faces;
On the faces of those still living, who
Hide their heads under blankets,
And on the faces of dead friends, who
Don't hide anymore.

Translated by Alan Sillitoe

Yehuda Amichai

From 'Jerusalem 1967'

On the Day of Atonement 1967 I put on
My dark festival clothes and went to the Old City
  of Jerusalem.
I stood a long time in front of the lowly shop of an
  Arab,
Not far from the Shechem Gate, a shop that had
Buttons and clasps and cotton-reels
Of all colours, and zips and buckles.
A rare light and many colours, like an Ark of the
  Law, opened.

In my heart I told him that my father
Also had a shop like that with buttons and cotton.
In my heart I explained to him all the decades
And causes and events, that set me here now,
While my father's shop lies burnt there, and he is
  buried here.

As I was finishing it was time for the Closing
  Prayer.
And he too pulled down his shutters and closed his
  door
And I with all the other worshippers went home.

Translated by A. C. Jacobs

Yehuda Amichai

All the generations

All past generations have donated me,
Piece by piece, to be built here in Jerusalem,
Immediately, like a synagogue or alms-house.
It's as if you have no choice.
My name is the name of my donors:
It's as if you have no choice.

I'm close to the age my father died.
My testament is lined and patchworked.
I must alter my life and my death
Each day to fulfil all the prophecies
Which foretold me, so that they don't prove false.
It's as if you have no choice.

I have passed the age of forty. Because of this
There are jobs for which I would not
Be accepted. If I'd been in Auschwitz
They wouldn't have let me work,
But would have instantly cremated me.
It's as if I had no choice.

Translated by Alan Sillitoe

Tuvia Ruebner

Among iron fragments

Among iron fragments and rusty dreams
I found you

lost in my astonished hands:
is this your face, your shoulders; this, the hair of
    night?

dark flame and sleepy mouth
the years have forgotten your eyes

they rose up around you
with the sharpness of spikes

the fine, white dust above you
in winds that rose and died

I found you
my wounded face in the wind and my arms open
    wide.

Translated by Robert Friend

Tuvia Ruebner

Document

I exist that I may say

This house is not a house,
a place to spread fishnet, a barren rock, fear
there beside the square, did I say square?
a paved
wilderness.

I exist that I may say

This way is not a way,
its paths wind round, ascend in dream-rust
from the wood, I walk
the sand hill there, who walks? I'd
walked with child steps, in a sun
of ruin, hands stretched out, asking,
walking and asking my Father and Mother

I exist that I may say

My father's history is coal,
ashes, wind
of my sister's in my hair blowing
back, back, night wind
in my day I exist that I may say
yes their night voices, yes their weeping, yes
the one astray in the house in their absence, falling
from the shadow of its walls
out of fear of my voice to say yes
in the empty space.

Translated by Harold Schimmel

T. Carmi

A view of Jerusalem

To Tamara

I
Soft light, green
of treetops – one green,
the fir; another,
the pine. A blue nest in the middle
for the morning bells – one bell
for the fir; another
for the pine.
　　That is what the eyes see,
that is what the ears hear
in the northern window. There is nothing,
nothing like Jerusalem,
in which this distance says
something obscure, muted
and explicit.
　　The birds see the sound,
my wife sees the birds,
and I cannot lie to her.
There is nothing.

2
Child, child, little flower,
can I already play with you at words?
If I say to you that mine is ours,
that the button opens and none can close,
that the flower closes and none can open –
　　come here beside me.
Even when the sun is shining,
walk in the middle of the street.
When the street-lamp is before us,
put your shadow in mine.
When the street-lamp is behind us,
your hand in mine.
　　Always be visible,
within range of eye and voice,
and I will teach you games of hide-and-seek.

3
Naked. Bone, stone, sky.
Sirens drain our blood,
air foams in the wake of their sound.
Open wide. Dust—blind—and ashes.
Windowpanes make room for eyes,
eyes for the sound of sirens.
That is all a man is now.
   Take off your clothes.
I have to touch you.
Now.

4
Everyone speaks in song:
thinks one thing,
and says another;
says one thing,
and thinks.

A winter landscape filled with clocks.
A man puts on his smile like a coat.
Don't look at the lining.

The mine is a name.
The raid is a door.
The trap is a part.
There is no thing
that does not compel its opposite.

A grammar of fears.
The rules—extremely sudden,
and it's hard to talk.

One thing is clear:
everyone plays.

And another thing:
you are no exception.

5
Now. Tomorrow will surely come,
in my window.
And the walls without a window?
The windows covered with stone?

My wife sees the birds
hidden,
her eyes wide open.
I see my wife:
in the noon of night,
a silver dome at her right hand;
in the dark of day,
at her left a dome of gold.

Sirens in the eyes
and stones from a wall.
(Flash of entangled horns
A nail glittering in the Roman sun.)
A stone rises
like a small cloud —
   child, child,
little hand,
can I already say to you Jerusalem,
soft light, tomorrow, another green.

(*after the Mahaneh Yehudah explosion, 1969*)

Translated by Stephen Mitchell

Avner Treinin

The day is coming

The age of the first crocus will never
return. Always move on.
Level by level, the crossing, then
bridge over bridge, curving and climbing
to be stopped at the wall. The edge
of the carport. This is the time
to switch off the motor, begin to go down.

Bricks block a window, that is,
someone has changed his mind, does not want
to see what he wanted so much at the start
and already he tries
to wipe out the error, a flower pot
still there, but simply undone
like a heavy bird suddenly gone.

A dog at our window. Dog tells dog.
But what's he to me, my neighbour removed on a
    stretcher   ·
even his name I don't know, when the balconies
were removed, the mint plants, a street facing
comfortable chairs. When man spoke to man,
someone could get there, could tell us
while his body was still warm.

The day is coming when heavy waters
from the sea will no longer spread
over a bright beach, a boy building temples
of sand, shell castles on tunnels
with rivers streaming. The day is coming,
already logs from forests of dark
nations, sticky pitch and oil spreading.

Jerusalem below is a field of olives
under house joined to house, a crocus
that can't break out of the asphalt,

tangle of roots, bones that no horn
can arouse. Jerusalem above
is smoke falling from concrete chimneys.
A shriek of sirens wakes us in the morning.

On the Mount of Quietude he will lead me among
    the nations.
A beating of drums, covered with deerskin.
The old world down to its bedrock. And what is
    the secret
of a bright morning in this alien city where I was
    born?
Three blacks and a cinnamon, kings of the earth.
Golden dome, crescent on cross, David
shields Israel in a morning of grapes.

At noon the town square is empty,
a swarm of robes cut through, makes me remember
what happened in Hebron. Locked in
green glass, bubbles we never will breathe.
Still I believe. As in a crystal ball
that tells fortunes, the heart of the grape
still shows through the clusters of Hebron.

Many omens and Muftis, their Holy War,
swear death on these infidels who multiply
cells to the tissue, the tents, the arab
at his wheel, the potter from Hebron – Elhalil
is Abraham, Ibrahim is
the beloved, the leader, come near,
coming near, the blood will stand up and cheer.

As if the sign were given
every alley swarms. They shall enter in
at the windows, they shall run
upon the wall, storm in the streets –

I, me, why have I forsaken me
to walk in the valley of Hinnom
for I fear evil.

Hour after hour they cried,
all at once stopped. I think
of the frozen lake, that someone
did walk on the water.
Something
has got to move.

Translated by Shirley Kaufman

Dennis Silk

The Y.M.H.A., Jerusalem

From *Guide to Jerusalem* (2nd edition)

Are there lessons at the Y.M.H.A. –
You can name for them the English beasts –
English lessons for the Hebrew children?

Grammar pays the grocer
Certainly, the light queerly
Finds your wicked hand on the board.

It starts from the left,
This hand, like all wicked intentions,
All hearts, does not know how an elephant
Runs in Hebrew.
It belongs to the other side
With their flags and forts.

Dennis Silk

Sleeping gun-crew

We worked for the Father up there,
pushing the daylight weight of his gun
round the half-circle of our patience.
Father, poor Father, we say,
at Lights-Out we scoop out
a fox-hole in the Mother.
(Father, poor Father, till washed
by such tears his wife allows.)

Adonai, poor Adonai,
in stretcher-sleep our brain grows,
our meat is your woe,
our language in earth,
we grow tall on the tubers
of the Mother of cordite,
Ashtoreth of the ammunition-boxes.

Dennis Silk

Big as a skull

Scary city cobbled with thought,
You coded your name
In the doodle of a cul-de-sac
For the easy daylight reader
To trip in the cracks.
I read it translated
On a moon-map, or striking matches.

Pinchas Sadeh

Finding the road to India

Finding the road to India, or breaking through the
  gates of Baghdad with my sword;
Weighing the deeds of man on the scales, or
  considering
The passing events;
Planting vineyards and eating their fruit, or
Casting my spirit before the infernal dogs
Of debit and credit, pleasures and honour;
Building houses, or dealing in fine silk, learning
  or teaching—
Truly all these are far from me.

Has not the close breath of Autumn already
  reached me?
Hence what more to me
Are Baghdad's turrets and the life of honour?
A voice is calling me from distant forests,
A voice from the nights heavy with dew, the voice
  of the wind
Passing in swift flight over seas and many lands.
A voice full of sweet purity, a voice full of dreamy
  love, a voice
Full of wild disgust at life.
The voice of approaching Autumn. A voice calls
  and says:
Is this a time to build, or a time to take women, or
  a time
To plant vineyards and eat their fruit?
For all is falling, all is falling.

Translated by Reuven Ben-Yosef

Aryeh Sivan

Forty years peace

Forty years peace. Forty years.
Forty years the fig trees
multiply and replenish
the earth, like women whose breasts
touch and get caught everywhere,
and they do not care.
Forty years men sleep with their women:
their breath long and peaceful
like the breath of flutes
in the reeds by small rivers.
They allow the light of
the moon to envelop them:
men walk in peace, like sleepwalkers,
in fields of vines and pinetrees.

Translated by Anthony Rudolf and Natan Zach

Aryeh Sivan

To Xanadu, which is Beth Shaul

A man or woman walking today
to Xanadu, which is Beth Shaul,
reaches the black
eagles, perched
on high cliffs, they hover
in closed circles,
like new widows, round
and round. You can walk there
for hours in a silence
that does not speak,
contemplating the stolen
child, and his mother
running after him on
the mountain, wailing
in a terrible voice.

Translated by Anthony Rudolf and Natan Zach

Moshe Ben Shaul

Remembrance

The woman laid down her bundle of wood in the
    right place and went away.
Then the wind played a tangle of overtures.
It was in a distant square. I drum on my knees
    trying to remember. It was
A boy. Near a fence. In town. A flock of
    nightingales flew away from honey-canes and
    flutes.
I'm still drumming on my knees. Soldiers. Can it
    be soldiers?
Gallops in the dust. The lucid buzz of hornets.
    Mist rises from the ground.
I drum, I must recall something. Must free myself
    of chains.
I repeat:
The woman laid down
Her bundle of wood in the right place
And went away.

Translated by Avraham Birman

Natan Zach

Sergeant Weiss

An everlasting flower
buds on your forehead.
Your cheeks nurture
unseen grubs. Rarely
is your name mentioned
except on manoeuvres. You move
through your flesh as though
through a sieve; my time is still
troubled by your hand
whose watch marks time
other than my own.

Until your arrival I
had thought it necessary
to hurry back to my task.

I don't know how you treat children now.
It is hard thinking of your face
when I am afraid. Events have moved on
as to a late reel of film
that may not be watched again.
In the desert, still, they
worship you, with their boots on.
The brambles bend themselves
down, remembering your orders.

Weiss, I do not know
how much time will pass
before I recall you,
suddenly restless.

Your way was right, perhaps.
In the house you have built
nothing presses itself on you
except cold, heat, hunger,
desire perhaps. Water will

not prosper round your eyes.
The oleander will
not sing through your tongue. Mother is dead;
you will not be a child again, Weiss.

In this continuing parody on people's fate
war manages one of its most convincing roles:
formed by the formless, it can hardly recognise
its image; surrounding you like a sea that pierces
the swimmer's flesh, rearing the waves. Your
    madness is
one of war's possibilities, not the worst.
You created a situation we must put up with.

In the delusions that leave no sign of their
    existence
but move in us, I see your eyes agape, sometimes,
like oases. We who were not able in these years
to shape the war into a thing we understand
remember you as a page written in lines close
    together,
hard to read, correct; spaces of time passed, not
    fulfilled.

Translated by Jon Silkin and Avraham Birman

Natan Zach

Against parting

My tailor is against parting.
That's why, he
said, he's not going away;
he doesn't want to part
from his one daughter. He's definitely
against parting.

Once, he parted from his wife, and
she he
saw no more of (Auschwitz).
Parted
from his three sisters and
these he never
saw (Buchenwald).
He once parted from his mother (his father
died of a fine, and ripe age). Now
he's against parting.

In Berlin he
was my father's kith and kin. They passed
a good time in
that Berlin. The time's passed. Now
he'll never leave. He's
most definitely
(my father's died)
against parting.

Translated by Jon Silkin

Natan Zach

Put your mind

Put your mind now to this shivering brown,
your fingers finely in the wind, as
you touch this tree. Green, it is even more deeply
green at the crown, the trunk a little eaten
away, and yet still greedily
it sucks the sap out of the ground
that no-one can see here in the city.
Touch and finger and attend. Breathe in
the light again and again, light every
cloud on its way. It passes. And night
will not delay.

Translated by Elaine Feinstein

Dan Pagis

Roll-call

He stands, cold in the morning wind,
stamping his feet, rubbing his hands,
death's diligent angel
who worked hard and rose in rank.
Suddenly he feels he has made a mistake. All eyes,
he checks again in his open book
the bodies waiting for him in formation,
a square within a square. Only I
am missing. I am a mistake.
I extinguish my eyes quickly; I erase my shadow.
Please God, let me not be missed, let the sum
add up without me.

Here, forever.

Translated by Robert Friend

Dan Pagis

Twenty years in the valley

And afterwards? I don't know.
Each of us fell
into his own forgetfulness.

The road has widened a lot. My armoured car
still lies on the side of it, upside down.
Sometimes at noon I gaze
through its burnt-out eyes. I don't remember
these cypresses.
New motorists go by,
trying to forget another war
and other dead,
quicker than us to die.

But sometimes a wind descends to us,
rustles a wreath
that has rolled into the valley,
plucks leaf after leaf of it, and queries:
Are they in love? Yes. No. Yes.
A little? No.
Very much?
No.
Too much.

Translated by Robert Friend

Dan Pagis

Lesson in the observatory

Observe. The world now appearing
at zero point zero one degree
was,
as far as is known, the only one
to violate the silence.

Of average size, it floated in a blue bubble:
and sometimes there were sea winds, clouds,
sometimes a house, maybe a kite, and children,
and here and there an angel,
or a large garden or a town.
Beneath them were the dead, and beneath *them*
    rock;
and beneath the rock the prison of fire.

Is this clear? I repeat: above,
there were clouds and cries,
air to air missiles, fire in the fields,
memory.
And beneath these, buried deep,
houses, children. What else?

The dot to one side? That, it seems,
is the one moon of that world.
It had extinguished itself some time before.

Translated by Robert Friend

Dan Pagis

Europe, late

Violins float in the sky,
and a straw hat. I beg your pardon,
what year is it?
Thirty-nine and a half, still awfully early,
you can turn off the radio.
I would like to introduce you to:
the sea breeze, the life of the party,
terribly mischievous,
whirling in a bell-skirt, slapping down
the worried newspapers: tango! tango!
And the park hums to itself:
   I kiss your dainty hand, madame,
   your hand as soft and elegant
   as a white suede glove. You'll see, madame,
   that everything will be all right,
   just heavenly – you wait and see.
   No it could never happen here,
   don't worry so – you'll see – it could

Translated by Stephen Mitchell

Moshe Dor

Fundamentals

This morning a train gave a long blare
and the fingers taking the pen trembled as if
   holding a snake.
Victories are not as simple as newspaper headlines
and the empty sleeve, the wounded sight
will not be replaced by shouting 'On your feet! Get
   going!'
Will you turn right or left, will you put on
a fur hat, will the beating of your heart alarm
your ears, like a sea?
I saw a pine and a cypress entwined
when the snow's love was crushing their branches.
The snow thawed and was forgotten and the trees
   stayed embraced,
half brown withered death,
half life greener than ever.
This morning a train gave a long blare
and the fingers taking the pen trembled as if
   holding a snake.
The tongue was stumbling over heavy syllables
as if it was groping for long lost landmarks.
It is no longer possible to pin a sun on the breast
like a red flower. The white-hot light scorching
the eyes and the victors' vehicles imprinting
mechanized patterns on dirt roads.
At night they tossed in their sleep, huddled under
   army blankets,
and like children, they learned by heart the
   fundamentals: this is a star ... this is a stone ...
this is my body breathing ...

Translated by John Batki

Moshe Dor

Notes for an Armenian biography

The zodiac does not encircle
the head of Astrik Bartevian, Armenian,
tailor, thin, large-eyed, sewing
his life into stitches here in

his home, an alley wholly
stone: not a river, no poplars
on its banks, and the old language
patch on patch. His chest sinks

as if he leans permanently to meditate
on hopelessness. He does not want payment
when the needle flies over the trousers.
The king does not pitch his tent

by the river, there even the eyes
of the crucified one become stones.
Sometimes, talking to the whore from
down the alley, listening more than speaking,

he flares slightly his nostrils
into the sweet dark perfume. A
very lonely man, who once dreamed
he weaved gold brocade for the archbishop's robe,

forgetting the elemental dictum of blackness,
who once in his dreaming sailed the boat
of the moon home, where he had never been,
where he wept between white peaks while

the grass flared like a green madness
on those slopes. Astrik
Bartevian, Armenian, when the thunderhead
of bells tears open around him, gives

thanks that his fate is ordained,
that he lives in a holy city and sews
with decaying fingers shrouds
for little stone birds.

Translated by Denis Johnson

Moshe Dor

War

*A light wind began blowing and brought
from a neighbouring field many flowers that
rained down all over the army until they
found themselves dripping with bouquets.*

Plutarch

In his helmet he is a black rose
growing toward battle where the flowers of blood
will engulf his eyes. Now only the blaze
out of his green youth turns his cheeks red.

The scabbard trembles to be emptied as the war
engages the colour of a sexual fantasy:
there is no current inventory of his desire,
we know only that he waits patiently, voluptuously

for the blowing of horns. From where he stood
the sling-stones, turning golden in the light,
seemed chrysanthemums lost from his childhood
and his shock at the sudden pain was slight.

The scribbled inventory of those hurt
–their numbers, units, living relations–
listed him among the first, and in the curt
military style offered itemization
of what he had that was theirs to take back.

In such epic cataloguing of the gear
and gashes of battalions there is some lack
of attention to poetry – sad, for it was clear

at the opening of battle that he was a black rose
and even clearer – blacker, more like a flower – at
   the close.

Translated by Denis Johnson

Moshe Dor

Wounds

Una cancion es una herida de amor
que nos abrieron las cosas.
Gabriela Mistral

The wounds of love
are healed.
The words
will be dulled.
The voice
will not make itself heard.

The wounds of metal
are real.
The withering
flower of someone's manhood
is flung across the wide starlessness.
The torn chest clutches
the flare-bomb, the words
retreating, stumbling, their eyes scarred.

The wounds of love have knit.
The wounds
of metal are fresh, the blood is like dew,
golden nightingales will grow calm
emerging from the storm in the arteries,
fluttering over the white virginity of bone.
The words will move into twilight.

Translated by Denis Johnson

Itamar Yaoz-Kest

A boy and a dream

Like frost
death spreads through his body.
The doors of the cabin are open,
the winter scene looms
in white silence
and he
on the wheels of his closed eyes
is borne away.

Translated by Uzi Nystar

David Avidan

Morning and evening march

Modified mirrors, photographic art, the film
    industry
and every possible invention
in one or any of these fields
enable you, better than your ancestors,
to view yourself from an outside angle.
The development of the street and of street
    language
allow you better than your ancestors
unhesitatingly to inject
into your most intimate random prayers
sentences like 'let yourself go'.
Well then, do it, let yourself go – only be careful
not to lose sight, not even for a moment,
of your outrageous visage and its swaying back
walking away from you forever,
with its terrible threat

never to let you rest.
Let yourself follow it, morning and evening,
midnight and noon. Do not
lose sight of it, in case you stumble
and get lost in the snow – if there is snow,
and in the desert – if there is desert.

Translated by Alan Sillitoe

David Avidan

The desert generation

Let fear break through.

Brave and solemn armadillos break through lush
     grass
to gaze on their first and last sun,
And realize better than you
The meaning of fate.

Let fear break through.

Let it come through in short cool volleys
Let it tear you to shreds. It will cool
Down long before you fragment,
Taking its chance and your own chance with it.

Let fear break through.

You realize fully you're one of the desert
     generation,
Can discover this sordid fact in the children's eyes
Who wander the glittering streets your father
Could have built
And which you some day luckily might raze.
Such reality will happen when you're gone.

Let fear break through.

You who were made to deny reality
Whose only reality lies in denial
Have caught yourself redhanded
Taking pity.

Let fear break through.

Wait for it bravely and with patience. Set
a cunning ambush. Lure
it slyly in. Don't

trust it. Stay awake. Don't
fall in love with sleep, or you'll
wake up destitute.

Let fear break through.

Let it move slowly like a desert army
Let it march agreeably within you, like fear in the
    desert:
You're one of the desert generation
Yet soon may hear a daring desert voice
tearing the lushest grass to scorching shreds.

Let fear break through.

For Man's but a plant of the field
And you are a plant of the field.
Do not attack fear in the field
For it comes on the wind's desire.

Let fear break through.

You'll soon forget all the words
You have ever spoken.
Night will pass like a dark efficient orderly
Inside a burning hospital
At some far-off battlefront
On which you had no opportunity to fight.

Let fear break through.

The morning after will be
Like all other mornings in all other deserts.
Fear will break through – without your permission –
But the desert generation will aim at the stars.

Translated by Alan Sillitoe

Moshe Hane'omi

Impressions of call-up

1
Evening. Walking in Beersheba
Before-after-during war.
People are buying watches and shoes.
Lots of money. Already it's cold.
In the department store you can get warm.

For many years there will pass through me
A feverish Yom Kippur
Of another kind.

For Aviva

2
What would I have done without you
When I came to Jerusalem.
My call-up girl,
Love of my war.
You kept the gentleness of your body
For me.

And when I came back home
You felt the gaps in my body.
The cold air, the desert,
The heat, the loathing.
You were soft and good
And accepted my scales
With love.

3
There are whole people in the restaurant.
They are still eyes and hands,
And clothes and hairstyles
And studying for M.A.s
A little girl goes to the toilet,
A big girl eats *tehina*.
And young men in suits come in
And order *shashlik* and hearts.
A boy comes in with his hat over his ears,
And one woman is on a diet.

We sat there at the end of the war
And drank red wine.
For a moment we thought nothing was different.

For a moment we thought nothing was different.

Translated by A. C. Jacobs

Israel Pincas

I see them moving off

And soon we'll have to roll up our bundles to trek
   a weary
road – this time where?
over snowy landscape, mountain
and forest, fields iced in,
I see them moving off
from me, each with his bundle, separate
straying in their night,
Father first and Brother, Mother behind him,
I feel the warm lover going slowly cool in my
   hands,
and the frothing sea calming inside me tamed.

Translated by Harold Schimmel

Dalya Ravikovich

In Jerusalem

And as if out of spite
at the funeral
(the sun was cruel even in winter)
I saw Ein Karem
the monastery and little gardens,
hills below hills
and hills above hills.
In the brush
a roof or two
of monasteries.
I know where he lives
but don't know where he is.
He's mostly not there
like a cloud that hides Jerusalem.

I want to be with him
in the light or in the dark
also in Jerusalem.
Need I say he's handsome?
It's so easy for me to praise him.
And as if out of spite
at the funeral
travelling from Ein Karem to the
cemetery hill
with so many cars
and so many mourners,
ropes fell from me
in pleasure,
I wanted to live still
maybe in Jerusalem.
But I exaggerate again.
I wanted him.

Translated by Harold Schimmel

Dalya Ravikovich

Hard winter

The little mulberry shook in the flame
and before its glory vanished
it was lapped in sadness.

Rain and sun ruled by turns, and in the house
we were afraid to think
what would become of us.

The plants reddened at their hearts
and the pool lay low.
Each of us was sunk in himself alone.

But for an instant, off-guard,
I saw
how men topple from this world

Like a tree that lightning splits
heavy with limbs and flesh, the wet branches
trampled like dead grass.

The shutter was worn and the walls thin.
Rain and sun, by turns, rode over us
with iron wheels.

All the fibres of the plants were intent
on themselves alone.
This time I never thought I'd survive.

Translated by Chana Bloch

Samih El-Kassim

Cinerama

1
In the next room clothes of a woman and a man
Scattered as in haste
And a whisper of tunes and strings of words
And in the window a strange bird nods its wings
Saying: I am the lover and the beloved.
And was gone. And didn't say. And didn't say
When my end will come.

2
No start of a song did they leave me to sing.
No splendour for my eyeballs.
Their laughter flows
When they hear me coaxing the winds
To uproot mountains.
O ancient dead – who will restore me
To the days of their might
For but a split moment.
Fade, imaginings!

3
In my aloneness I'll let the sadnesses
Shake the ashes of my sorrows
Expel the smoke
From the sparks of my embers, revealing
My human account without deceptions
Then bells will sound inside my heart.

*Translated from the Arabic by Sasson Somekh and
Richard Flantz*

Meir Wieseltier

It's hard to teach a child

Slowly slowly, children learn to hate.
It takes them lots of time, many
years at school, to teach a child to hate
is no simple task. Every teacher knows
how the love in them refuses to melt,
starts to crumble, leaves an insipid taste
in the preaching mouth. Sometimes a child learns
to bear his enemies on his shoulders,
struggles some distance, stumbles, rises and brings
    down
a rain of wonder
and hope onto bald heads.
He's encircled, but still doesn't know. In pounding
    innocence
he thrusts out his heroic lips and sucks
his foe's contaminated blood.
With his doom already known he stretches a final
    hand
into the womb of the world, to be sunk,
to be absorbed again.
It's hard to teach a child.

Translated by Avraham Birman and Richard Flantz

Meir Wieseltier

A dream of death as an angel

People wearing white linen robes
eating olives and sesame
reading scrolls
in walled cities
in forests
on pillows on stone,

dreamed the day of their passing
in the shape of an angel who comes
from the wall or tree
the knife
in his hand
makes explanations superfluous.

They go with him they don't complain
or they ask wait awhile
till I make provisions for my household
till I finish
my work
then you'll lay your hand on me.

And in special cases
found in the writings
it's possible to debate with him
to say you're early
go and return
in a couple of months, in a year,

for even an angel of destruction like him
retreats when he's faced with the facts
with a truth about life
nor dares
to presume
if there's substance in what a man says:

he goes as he came
returns some other time
from the wall or tree
the gleam from the knife
in his hand
shines like the shining of heaven.

Translated by Shirley Kaufman and Shlomit Rimmon

Yair Hurwitz

Whispering in me

The dead man took hold of me.
I followed him.
He appeared to me at night – that dead man.
I followed his years.

He was a kingdom once.
Years passed.
A cracked halo crowned him.
A broken light moved in me.
I know those difficult days.

A man is walking in the street.
He sees me laugh – that man.
But how can I explain
that someone dead has me in his grip
and magic spells
whisper powerful in me?

Translated by S. F. Chyet and Leonore Gordon

Chaim Be'er

The sequence of generations

I am a child
of six generations here
under the sun of Lower Syria.
Mother and my aunts
during the World War
eat grass
and go begging for
colonial merchandise —
little girls trapped
in poverty,
waiting for General Allenby,
a commander who is more like Wellington
than Napoleon,
an Englishman who spent the last decade of his life
studying the lives of birds
and taking long trips,
getting down from his horse at Jaffa Gate,
and in the Street of the Patriarchs
the heathens say to them
Return return O Shulamite,
eyes on them from every side.
Return that we may look upon thee,
and they run away and answer
What will ye see in the Shulamite,
hungry little girls in checkered blouses
who remind them of
the lady Mary, a Semitic woman
in Terra Sancta,
and I am a child
little by little
in the world of actions
building the family tree,
always as if walking
in happy light.
There is nothing more enchanting in life than this,
to sit in the crusader East

and to see the sheep scattered upon the hills
and only the Lamb of God
standing and weeping –
Dominus flevit – the Lord
in his Byzantine beauty
standing and weeping
on Mount of Olives
as he comes from Bethany,
and on the threshing floor of Aravna the Jebusite
already the Mother of Zion hears
words of a husband to his wife
and laughs.
Praise is comely.

Translated by Stephen Mitchell

Yisrael Hame'iri

In a plane from Refidim to Lydda

I wouldn't have believed it. How the desert
    suddenly became distant,
And the dug-in vehicles of destruction grew smaller
    and smaller
And the earth began moving slowly, circling as in a
    dream,
And a strange, icy wind blew, and darkness came
    slowly down,
And stars appeared between the clouds, quite
    clearly stars,
And the heart took off in craziness and wouldn't
    believe it,
Didn't want to believe it (or perhaps couldn't), and
    fell asleep
For a moment, and then came the hard, dry blow
    of landing.

Translated by A. C. Jacobs

Siham Dawoud

1
The wind is racing with the train
And oranges are sleeping in my arms.
Tears descend from my mother's eyes
And through the windows of my wounds
Time waits to kill me.

2
Stepping down, I saw you out of a new land,
Standing with your lover, who was rain,
To meet me from the funeral,
A pomegranate seed which was your history,
The sun's coin, rain, wind from the east:
My sign had stopped travelling,
Made from my flesh and your skin
An offering for birds – a nail
To shield us from the squally west.

3
When without desire I ran naked to you
I forgot the policeman who had
Disfigured you, altered the colour
Of our oranges. But I told you
From my lung:
They cannot rob the olives of their green –
For the tears I shed, like the colour of your eyes,
Are green.

Translated by Alan Sillitoe

Be'eri Hazak

Lord of the universe

I beseech thee: turn up the volume of your
   transmitter.
Here, I
Do not hear, do not know, if
You have once more stuck an iron flower in the
   buttonhole
Of your aerial. You are so gentle. Why
Are you so benign. Why are you always
So polite. *How do you read me? Over. Over.* I hear
   you brokenly, as if
You are wounded, you

In the surrounded valley. Different mountains
Another Galilee. I beseech thee,
Let me know the volume of your signals; your face
   won't focus
On the radar screen, why
Aren't you tank-tracked, why aren't you
Fighting, shall I send a motorized patrol. I am
So full of faith
That it would not reach you nor get back to me.
   Black
Wound. I beseech thee, turn down
The volume of your signals.
The tops of the cypresses at evening
Whisper your name in vain, and where would the
   lonely Pole
Star guide your chariot host
Where would it guide the—
I beseech thee, close your eyes. I read you
Now *Roger*. You can die
At last. Bereaved father, I already cease
To feel.
Winter tears will say Kaddish over you.

Translated by Aharon Megged and Alan Sillitoe

Be'eri Hazak

Private forest

Surely the host of angels always sails in your ships.
When will it cross my days,
When will it come to shore?

You turn to my smile but I shall keep your tear.
And wound will cleave to wound.

My years are travelling towards their end,
And in the fenced-off forest of my memories
A hard pain will break from a soft pain.
Your angels are not mine, not yours.

And what will be left?
Whispering embers. The quiver of your voice.
No more.

Translated by Aharon Megged and Alan Sillitoe

Be'eri Hazak

Moses brought forth water from the rock by his
   feet.
Men are silently resting now.
If his shoes had been soldered
To his feet, perhaps
He would not have brought forth
Such water
That did not stop flowing
At the picture of his smile.

Moses brought forth water and men are mute
Like the rock at whose feet
They now lie. And later
I wondered why the rocks
Are so hard in 1970-men
Who rest so quietly.

But Moses brought forth water from the rock
And did not turn pale and did not shout:
Since then the water covers
Isaac's green eyes.

Translated by Aharon Megged and Alan Sillitoe

Be'eri Hazak

Why are you so shaken, father,
Silent father, you who are
Filled with your shout?
My clenched hand is at your hair, I
Who am your pains
To come.

How shall I not remember
That with tears you have sown me
And with weeping you will reap me.

Translated by Aharon Megged and Alan Sillitoe

INDEX OF FIRST LINES

INDEX OF TITLES